T0371875

CLOUD
SPOTTING

Observe the Clouds
to Quiet Your Mind

By Casey Schreiner

Cover Art by Margaret Jeane
Interior Illustrations by Liana Jegers

CLOUD
SPOTTING

CHRONICLE BOOKS
SAN FRANCISCO

POCKET NATURE

Text copyright © 2022 by **CASEY SCHREINER**.

Library of Congress Cataloging-in-Publication Data available.

ISBN 978-1-7972-1824-3

Manufactured in China.

Series concept and editing by **CLAIRE GILHULY**.
Series design by **LIZZIE VAUGHAN**.
Cover art by **MARGARET JEANE**.
Interior illustrations by **LIANA JEGERS**.

Typeset in Albra, Benton Sans, Caslon.

10 9 8 7 6 5 4 3

Chronicle books and gifts are available at special quantity discounts to corporations, professional associations, literacy programs, and other organizations. For details and discount information, please contact our premiums department at corporatesales@chroniclebooks.com or at 1-800-759-0190.

Chronicle Books LLC
680 Second Street
San Francisco, California 94107
www.chroniclebooks.com

CONTENTS

Clouds come **FLOATING**
into my life, no longer
to **CARRY RAIN** or usher storm,
but to add color to my
sunset **SKY**.

—Rabindranath Tagore, *Stray Birds*

INTRODUCTION

What, exactly, is cloud spotting? Is it about recognizing all the different types of clouds? Sure, if you want it to be. There are ten basic types of clouds. Those cloud types also have subsets, called species and varieties (which all have names in Latin, naturally), if you want to get more precise. And of course, there are even more types of unique cloud phenomena and accessory clouds that have their own names too.

But you don't need to know all or any of that to partake in cloud spotting. Do you think that cloud looks like a rooster? Hey, that's cloud spotting.

Is cloud spotting about "collecting" types of clouds, or checking them off a list? Sure, you can get yourself a checklist of cloud types and try to hunt them all down. Lots of cloud spotters have a great time with that, the same way some hikers have peakbagging lists or runners try to qualify for their bucket list races. Humans love making lists for things. But it's not necessary.

Is it just about looking at clouds then? Well, yes, it's about looking at clouds. But more than that, it's about *noticing* clouds. What does the cloud look like? How is the light hitting it? Is it changing? If so, what is it changing into? How long will it last? Are there other types of clouds around or above it?

So, as a bona fide cloud spotter, you can be a Latin-speaking meteorologist . . . or you can just look up at the sky. You don't have to spend any money to cloud-watch. You can do it whenever you want for as long as you want, from just about anywhere in the world. Those aren't things you can say about too many other hobbies.

Another great aspect of cloud spotting is that it can be an accessible gateway into approaching mindfulness, whether as part of a focused meditation or just a contemplative outdoor activity that allows your mind to wander.

Much has been said about mindfulness lately, and it has become somewhat of an empty buzzword used to sell products or lifestyle programs. But at its core, mindfulness simply means being fully present in a moment without being distracted and without judgement.

Sounds easy, right? OK, give this a go, then: Save your page here, put this book down, close your eyes, and pay attention only to your breathing. Don't try to control it or try to change it—just notice it.

. . .

So how long did you last before your mind wandered off somewhere else? Don't worry—even long-practicing meditators find this challenging. Our brains have evolved to learn from past events and to try to predict the future, which is why when we *do* try to just be in the present, we end up replaying old, embarrassing conversations or planning for a project that's due next week.

Not to worry, though—it helps to have something to focus on. Some meditators use their breath. Others may use a prayer or mantra. Cloud spotters can use clouds.

Most of the time, we probably don't pay much attention to clouds. Unless they're pouring down rain or snow or blocking out the sun on our planned beach day, they usually just glide along in the background unnoticed. Sure, your eye may occasionally be drawn to clouds because of a spectacular sunset or beam of sunlight shining through, but everyday background clouds are just as deserving of our attention.

These huge and heavy (an average-size cumulus cloud can weigh over 1 million pounds [453,592 kg]!) masses of water droplets and ice are, like all things, in a state of constant flux. It is very possible for you to sit down with your eyes cast on the horizon and watch the birth, life, and death of a cloud formation in just a few moments. That acknowledgement of the transient nature of all things is a very important part of mindfulness meditation—and goes a long way in healing our over-frayed nerves in a world of constant agitations, obligations, and notifications.

The purpose of this book is to help you use what is freely available to you in nature to bring some mindfulness into your life. Along the way, you will learn a bit about the main types of clouds, as well as some of the more unusual cloud forms. You'll also learn some Latin, if you're into that sort of thing, and you'll learn a bit about what certain types of clouds may be able to tell you about incoming weather.

But most importantly, you will start to appreciate truly wonderful things that you may not have given much notice before. And all you have to do to get started is look up.

Nature is a
MUTABLE cloud,
which is **ALWAYS**
and **NEVER** the same.

—**Ralph Waldo Emerson,** "History"

I.

BENEFITS OF MINDFULNESS

This book will help you utilize the world around you to engage in a mindfulness practice. By taking just a few minutes out of your day to observe and notice the clouds, you can quiet your mind and tap into a mindful, meditative state. The concept of mindfulness is a seemingly simple one—pay attention to your current observations and experiences and accept them without any sort of judgment. Like many things, that's easier said than done—but it's definitely worth the attempt.

In recent years, Western medicine and psychology have begun to examine the benefits of mindfulness practices. For people who tend to ruminate, a mindfulness practice was found to be more effective than distractions in reducing negative thinking. Mindfulness has also been found to increase positive emotions and appreciation in people who are experiencing depression, decrease both short- and long-term anxiety, and even lower rates of job burnout and increase feelings of worthiness in workplaces.

Physiologically, new research also shows that mindfulness can improve heart health by lowering your blood pressure and heart rate, and it can even increase your chances of surviving a heart attack. A steady practice may also decrease cognitive decline due to aging and Alzheimer's, as well as slow the process of cellular aging. Other studies have shown that mindfulness can boost your immune system responses and keep inflammation under control. And in a world where chronic pain seems to be on the rise, mindfulness can offer both short- and long-term relief—even where surgeries and prescription painkillers have failed.

These are all pretty strong benefits for a practice that only asks you to take the time to be present in the moment and doesn't require monthly subscription fees or insurance co-pays.

While any mindfulness practice offers these myriad health benefits, there are even *more* benefits to using an experience in nature to tap into mindful thinking. Although these types of studies are new as well, we have begun to see that being in or even looking at pictures of nature can reduce anger, fear, and stress, lower blood pressure, improve memory functions and focus, spur creative thought, and even alter your sense of time so that you feel less rushed and more altruistic. Clouds—with their fleeting and ever-changing nature—and cloud watching—a mostly outdoor activity— offer an easy way to meditate in nature.

Psychology professor and author Alison Gopnik has written about the ways children come to know the world around them. In her work, she maps the way our scope of attention changes as we age. As toddlers and children, our consciousness is open to all sorts of input. But as we grow older, we tend to focus on a

few things we deem important—in the process, ignoring much of the world and allowing its stimuli to batter our unconsciousness.
According to Gopnik, "As we know more, we
see less."

Gopnik uses the terms *lantern* and *spotlight
attention* to describe these two ways of seeing
the world. Lanterns cast their illuminating
light in all directions, while spotlights limit
the amount of light they send out to a single
place. For Gopnik, lantern attention provides
a more holistic view of the world around you,
which can lead to more innovative and creative
thinking. Spotlight attention, on the other
hand, may provide focus on a single area but
risks obscuring connections with the rest of the
environment. We have also begun to find that
spending time in states of unfocused lantern
attention can provide many of the same benefits of mindfulness practices. And as luck would
have it, some of the best settings for getting us
into that lantern attention state are the ones we
find in the natural world.

Think about the way you pay attention to things in your life—when you're walking in a park or just enjoying the clouds in the sky, your attention likely wanders. Your sense of time slows down. Your heart rate and breathing decrease. Stress levels diminish. Compare that with the way you likely feel when you experience a moment of classic, demanding spotlight attention—like when you receive a wave of notifications on your phone.

When cloud spotting, it's OK to notice specific parts of cloud formations—that's how we'll learn to identify different cloud types. Just remember to also allow your eyes and mind to drift so you can shift into a state of lantern attention and open yourself up to mindfulness too.

O it is pleasant,
with a heart at ease,
Just after sunset,
or by <u>**MOONLIGHT SKIES**</u>,
To make the <u>**SHIFTING CLOUDS**</u>
be what you please.

—**Samuel Taylor Coleridge,** "Fancy in Nubibus"

II.

WHAT IS A CLOUD?

Before we venture too far into the world of cloud spotting, it may be helpful to answer perhaps the most rudimentary question: What, exactly, is a cloud?

We've all seen them. We all know them. We've all likely let their very existence slide into our daily backdrops without even noticing it.

Clouds are, at their simplest, invisible water vapor that has evaporated from a source of liquid water. In its gaseous form, water vapor can hold and transfer heat into the air. Air can only hold a set amount of water vapor, though. If the air is warm or the region is under the influence of a high pressure weather system, it can hold more.

If an area of warm, high pressure air suddenly becomes cooler or lower in pressure, then the water vapor it holds will either turn back into liquid in a process called condensation (the same process you see when you bring a glass of iced tea into a humid summer backyard and water appears on the outside of the glass), or the vapor will turn into a solid as ice in a process called deposition. These shifts in temperature and pressure can occur in numerous ways. Perhaps a cold or warm front moves into the area. Or the path of a jet stream alters and sends high-speed winds into a region. Or sometimes, it's as simple as air being forced upward by a hill or mountain.

For water vapor to make the transition into a liquid or solid, it requires a non-gaseous surface to condense. These tiny particles are called cloud condensation nuclei, and they can be dust or sand, ash from volcanoes or wildfires, salt crystals from an ocean breeze, air pollution, or sometimes even bacteria. When there are enough condensation nuclei in the sky, water droplets or ice crystals will form, and when enough of these droplets or crystals form in the sky, that's what we call a cloud.

As we will learn, there are many types of clouds. Some produce rain or snow, others do not. Some float aimlessly in the sky, swept away by high force winds, while others create their own internal engines and can generate more clouds or exhaust themselves into nothingness. Some will smother the sky in uniform drabness; others may give you the opportunity to see some dazzling and otherworldly visual effects. Noticing some types of clouds or cloud progressions may even help you predict the future—or at least the weather of the future.

Clouds help move heat, water, and even dust and sand all around the planet. In fact, in 2015, NASA found one of the primary fertilizers in the Amazon rainforest was the phosphorus transported in dust from the Sahara Desert in northern Africa. Our world is much more interconnected than most of us think it is—and its incredible systems are hidden in plain sight. We just have to open our eyes and know where to look.

<HOW TO>

CLASSIFY CLOUDS

During the Age of Enlightenment, Western thinkers put their minds to making sense of the world. For better or worse, European scientists and philosophers began describing the world they sensed, searching for rational meaning, systems, and ways to organize and divide it.

The Swedish botanist, physician, and zoologist Carl Linnaeus published *Systema Naturae* in 1735. This was the first book to consistently use the Latin naming system for plants and animals we still use today, dividing the world into kingdoms, phylums, classes, orders, family, genera, and species (Linnaeus also proposed a similar system for classifying minerals, but that one didn't stick).

Linnaeus oversaw twelve editions of this book, which was unbelievably influential in European scientific circles. In 1803, the British chemist and amateur meteorologist Luke Howard self-published an essay called *On the Modifications of Clouds* that took much inspiration from Linnaeus. In the essay, Howard used Latin terms to describe some of the basic forms of clouds as well as acknowledge and describe the common transitional forms that occur as clouds change.

Howard's essay was something of a viral hit, traveling through Quaker and scientific communities and even winning a very vocal fan in the famous German poet Johann Wolfgang von Goethe—who not only wrote the young amateur scientist some effusive fan mail, but also contributed poems about the cloud types for future editions of the essay.

The foundations of Howard's system are still in use today, and they were instrumental in advancing the fields of meteorology and climate science. However, these days, few of us can be considered amateur scientists, and even fewer are versed in the language of Latin.

Although this book will use and acknowledge a lot of Latin names in the following pages, you *really* only need to grasp a few basic terms to wrap your head around the scientific names of clouds.

LET'S LEARN SOME LATIN

Cirrus

Means "a lock of hair" or "horsehair," and describes clouds with a thin, delicate, wispy appearance.

Cumulus

Means "an accumulation," "pile," or "heap," and describes clouds with flat bottoms and large, puffy tops.

Nimbus

Literally means "rain cloud," and is applied to clouds that produce precipitation.

Stratus

Comes from the verb meaning "to flatten out or cover in a layer" and describes clouds that are generally short but spread out over a large area.

The basic types of clouds are all combinations of these terms, sometimes mixed with the prefix *alto*, which just means "above" or "at a greater height." If you know those five terms, you've basically got the ten common cloud types down! What's a cirrostratus? Well, it's a thin wispy cloud that's spread out over a large area. Stratocumulus? That's a whole bunch of flat-bottomed puffy clouds all bunched up together. Cumulonimbus? That's a rather large, flat-bottomed puffy cloud that's about to dump some rain. See? It's not as tough as it looks at first glance.

Those basic cloud types are the genus of each cloud (think of the genus as the most general grouping). The cloud types all have species and variety names as well, to more specifically define the cloud being observed (species is more specific than genus; variety is like an additional description and is not always needed or used). Not every cloud genus has every species and variety, though, and sometimes a cloud may not have the distinctions that indicate a specific species or variety, and can just be known as its genus. We'll get into the varieties in the individual cloud type entries later on, but if you want to learn a little more Latin, here are the species you'll find.

Calvus

Meaning "bald." The upper parts of these clouds appear smooth with flattened mounds.

Capillatus

Meaning "having hair." The upper parts of these clouds have fibrous elements that look like a mess of uncombed white hair.

Castellanus

From the word for "castle" or "fortifications." Formations in this species tend to have tall towers or turret formations on their tops.

Congestus

Meaning "piled up" or "accumulated." These clouds appear taller than they are wide.

Fibratus

Meaning "fibrous." These clouds display distinct, often parallel formations in curves or straight lines.

Floccus

From the term for "a tuft of wool" or "cloth." These clouds are puffy with ragged bases and sometimes have formations stretching from beneath them.

Fractus

From the word for "broken" or "shattered." These clouds have torn-up, ragged edges.

Humilis

Meaning "small" or "low to the ground." These clouds appear wider than they are tall.

Lenticularis

Meaning "like a lentil." This describes clouds that appear with a smooth lens or lentil shape.

Mediocris

Meaning "in the middle" or "medium." These clouds are about as tall as they are wide.

Nebulosis

Meaning "nebulous" or "covered in fog or mist." This is used when a cloud is a large, gray, generally indistinct layer.

Spissatus

From the verb meaning "made thicker" or "condensed." This is generally used when more delicate cloud forms clump up into a larger, more dense version.

Stratiformis

Meaning (generally) "looking spread out or flattened and covered with a layer." This is used when a cloud formation spreads over a large area.

Uncinus

Meaning "hooked." These are clouds that literally have a hook shape to them.

I am the
DAUGHTER OF EARTH AND WATER,
And the nursling of the SKY;
I pass through the pores
OF THE OCEAN AND SHORES;
I change, but I cannot die.
For AFTER THE RAIN when with
never a stain
The PAVILION OF HEAVEN is bare,
And THE WINDS AND SUNBEAMS
with their convex gleams
Build up THE BLUE DOME OF AIR,
I silently laugh at my own
cenotaph,
And out of THE CAVERNS OF RAIN,
Like a child from the womb,
like a ghost from the tomb,
I ARISE and unbuild it again.

—Percy Bysshe Shelley, "The Cloud"

III.

TYPES OF CLOUDS

There may be countless clouds in the sky, but almost all of them can be classified as one of ten common types. In this section, we will move from clouds at the lowest elevation to the highest (with a slight detour for one cloud—the overachieving cumulonimbus—that occupies low, medium, and high elevations all at once!). We will learn about each type of cloud and how we can observe them on their own terms.

TYPES OF CLOUDS

HIGH

CIRRUS

CIRROSTRATU

- -

MIDDLE

ALTOSTRATUS

- -

LOW

NIMBOSTRATUS

STRATOCUMULUS

STRATUS

CIRROCUMULUS

ALTOCUMULUS

CUMULONIMBUS

CUMULUS

STRATUS

You wake up, ready to face the day. You turn on some lights, stretch out a bit, then head to your window to see what weather you'll be enjoying today. What you see is gray. *Lots* of gray. Your first reaction may be to sigh or think about crawling back into bed, but instead, you may just want to say, "Good morning, stratus clouds."

Stratus clouds have been described as "uniformly gray," "featureless," "extending for miles," and "boring." They are the clouds that form closest to the ground and are most commonly found around coastlines and mountains, where moist air cools over a surface (whether land or water) that's colder than its surroundings. A stratus cloud that touches the ground is what we call fog, although there is some debate about whether or not fog is technically a cloud at all—the United States National Weather Service defines fog as "visible moisture that begins at a height lower than 50 feet (15 m)." Anything above 50 feet? A cloud. Even though it's the same stuff.

Stratus clouds show up in two different species. The most common is known as *Stratus nebulosus,* which forms a flat and featureless layer. Slightly tougher to distinguish is the *Stratus fractus*, which basically describes what happens when that flat and featureless layer starts to dissipate and break into shreds—which can sometimes happen underneath other larger clouds.

Cloud spotters also have a few varieties to describe stratus clouds: *opacus*, which is when the layer is thick enough to obscure the sun or moon; and *translucidus*, which is when you can see vague outlines of the sun and moon. Although, either way, they're still mostly just a large layer of gray.

In addition to being huge and indistinct, stratus clouds never seem to be in much of a hurry to do anything. They take a long time to form—usually overnight—and because they form when the atmosphere is in fairly stable layers, they tend to linger around through at least the late afternoon if they end up dissipating at all.

So where is the silver lining in this massive blanket that seems to smother out all sunlight from an otherwise lovely day? Like many things, this one just requires a slight change of perspective.

Along coastal regions with nearby mountains, thick stratus clouds make regular appearances at certain times of the year. They are often referred to as "the marine layer" (even though this technically describes the inversion layer and not the clouds themselves), and they have fooled many an early-riser into thinking there is no sunshine to be had.

However, because these clouds are so low, it is possible to get above them. Which, of course, means you get to actually go *through* them. Unless you count taking off in an airplane, stratus clouds are likely to be the only cloud you can stand inside. When making your way through stratus clouds, you may feel completely suspended in air, with little sensory input to guide you. Was that sound nearby or far away?

If you keep climbing, though, you may have a chance to break through the stratus layer. Once there, you may be treated to a pure blue sky overhead and a sweeping view of the stratus layer blanketing the valleys below. In Southern California, this phenomenon is sometimes called "the Phantom Sea" because it's easy to imagine you're on an elevated shoreline while clouds crash against the coast in exquisite slow motion. I used to consider this term a somewhat artistic interpretation of an ocean, but a few years back, people started posting sped-up time-lapse videos of these stratus clouds crashing against the San Gabriel and Santa Monica Mountains, and you know what? It really does look like an active coastline. So much for boring, right?

MINDFUL REFLECTION

Sometimes perspective can make a big difference in how we feel about things. Think about something that happened to you recently. How would the "you of five years ago" have experienced this moment? How do you think the "you of five years from now" might experience it?

CUMULUS

Picture a perfectly clear blue sky. It's a sunny day. The wind is light—a breeze gently tousles your hair, but not enough to make you worry about throwing on another layer of clothing.

Now picture *the perfect* cloud in the sky. Let me guess—it's puffy; it almost looks like you can reach out and pull a few strands of cotton from it. Perhaps the base is flat. Perhaps there are a few companion clouds, but each one is separate and distinct. They're brilliant white, like someone colored in the rest of the sky cobalt but intentionally left these spaces blank. Are you hearing the opening notes to the theme song from *The Simpsons*?

You are looking at a cumulus cloud.

Perhaps because these clouds are so common, or perhaps because they mostly signal fair weather, they have become sort of a default symbol for clouds themselves. If the weather app on your phone shows a cloudy day in the forecast, odds are the icon is a cumulus cloud. Did your niece draw you a cute picture of the two of you playing outside? If there's a cloud in the sky, it's probably a cumulus.

Cumulus clouds are individual formations that take shape via rising thermals—updrafts of warmer air caused by the sun heating the ground below. These clouds form above land, and float peacefully by at low altitudes (most often 1,000 to 5,000 feet [300 to 1,500 m]).

If you watch them carefully throughout the day, you may see them grow vertically, fed by those rising columns of warm air, as if adding new layers of frosting on top of their already massive forms. The four main subspecies of cumulus clouds follow that growth as they gather up more moisture over time, and eventually dissipate. If you're patient, you may get to watch these transitions in slow real time.

Cumulus humilis are usually first to show up. They appear wider than they are tall and a bit on the flat side, and can provide a good amount of shade if there are enough of them around. These are those *Simpsons* clouds you likely pictured.

Cumulus mediocris are about as tall as they are wide, and will show up later in the afternoon if the *humilis* clouds continue to be built up by thermals.

If a cumulus cloud has been floating around for a while gobbling up heat and moisture, it may get significantly taller than it is wide. Its base will likely darken. At this point, it's a *Cumulus congestus*—and you might want to be on the lookout for rain. These tall cumulus clouds can look supremely majestic, and almost prismatic when the sun hits them at the right angle. Walk through an art gallery of Western paintings and you're likely to see these towers off in the distance. Congestus clouds that keep growing may turn into cumulonimbus clouds, which are a separate kind of cloud we'll talk about later.

But if you're watching a cumulus cloud in stable air, you may also see it begin to break down while losing heat and dissolve back into invisible water vapor. A cumulus cloud that looks like a cotton ball that's being slowly torn asunder by unseen hands is known as *Cumulus fractus*. These are likely to show up toward the end of the day, straining to provide shade from a relentless sun, and can sometimes be found beneath rain clouds as well.

CUMULUS

MINDFUL REFLECTION

Moments of intense beauty—like a sky full of perfect cumulus clouds—can be exceptionally fleeting in our lives. Remember to appreciate each moment on its own terms. Try not to get attached to beauty, or avoid drabness or ugliness.

STRATOCUMULUS

In the morning, you look out your window and see a low, uniform gray blanket of stratus clouds (page 40). You go about your routine—fire up a cup of tea or coffee, sit down for breakfast, maybe catch up on some reading. You notice a tiny sunbeam illuminate part of your book. If you look back up at the sky and notice that uniform gray starting to break up into clumps with maybe a bit of blue sky peeking through, you have just witnessed the transition from stratus to stratocumulus.

Stratocumulus clouds are found worldwide at low elevations and are very common. They usually form from a layer of stratus clouds being broken up by weak convective air currents and are prevented from growing into the taller cumulus clouds by a dry, stable layer above—or by a group of cumulus clouds that move close enough together to cover the sky. You'll be able to tell the difference between a stratocumulus layer and a stratus layer because the former has a lot more variation in its tones, even though they're both gray. The stratus tends to be fairly monochromatic, while a stratocumulus will show off all kinds of shades, from dark gray to nearly white.

Stratocumulus clouds come in three main species: *Stratocumulus stratiformus* is a layer of stratocumulus that covers the entire sky. *Stratocumulus lenticularis* are strange-looking, disc-shaped clouds that appear when a moist airstream travels above raised terrain like a hill or mountain in a stable atmosphere. When the top of a stratocumulus cloud is covered in what appear to be tiny, upward-stretching strings or turrets, it's known as a *Stratocumulus castellanus*. These can sometimes continue growing upward into *Cumulus congestus* clouds, which are likely to drop a bit of precipitation.

Don't worry too much about trying to label these clouds, though—stratocumulus clouds show the most variation amongst the lower cloud formations, so if one of those species descriptions isn't immediately obvious to you, you can just go ahead and call it simply "stratocumulus."

Beyond their impressive range of gray-scale presentations, stratocumulus clouds are also the primary type of cloud known to cause crepuscular rays—those gorgeous, awe-inspiring orange sunbeams that appear to radiate from stratocumulus clouds at twilight when the sun is below the horizon.

So if you are observing stratocumulus clouds, between their varying colors, the different types and formations, and the way they filter light, you will surely have a lot to observe.

STRATOCUMULUS

MINDFUL
REFLECTION

Set aside some time today to
observe an object or area for
a much longer time than you
would otherwise. How does
it change? Can you tell what
causes that change? What
else changes around it? Try
not to assign values to those
changes—just observe them
for what they are.

NIMBOSTRATUS

The nimbostratus cloud is a fairly easy one to identify, although perhaps it is not the most visually exciting. They are low, thick, gray, mostly featureless clouds that block all light from the sun or moon above. And they produce rain or snow. In fact, nimbostratus clouds are one of two cloud types *defined* as producing rain, along with the towering cumulonimbus (page 69). But while cumulonimbus clouds are monstrous and exciting, dumping heavy rainstorms in a short period of time, nimbostratus clouds linger for hours, can extend in a thick layer over thousands of square miles, and drop a steadier, longer-lasting precipitation.

Nimbostratus clouds generally form when a higher altostratus takes on moisture from an advancing warm front and lowers in elevation. Because its shape is so indistinct, the nimbostratus has no species or varieties. It's just "nimbostratus."

With all this said, you may be wondering what you could possibly observe when a big nimbostratus layer rolls into town, hiding the sun and maybe giving you an excuse not to go running in the morning. Well, remember that the purpose of mindful cloud spotting is to observe cloud phenomena without judgement; but also, in the case of this particular cloud, it's not so much about noticing the cloud itself but rather the cloud's effects.

Imagine, at this very moment, you're cozied up indoors while a massive nimbostratus sits directly above your home. In any direction you look, the sky is a surprisingly uniform gray. Rain is falling now, creating percussive beats on the roof just over your head. Perhaps you can see drops striking the trees and plants just outside your window, giving the just-turning leaves a reflective glaze.

Looking toward the street, the rain from our good friend the nimbostratus runs down a slope past the exhausted garden but soaks in the ground where you planted some native meadow seeds just a few weeks ago. Because nimbostratus clouds provide gentle, steady rain instead of the rushing downpours of cumulonimbus clouds, it's not hyperbolic to say that nimbostratus clouds literally bring life-giving water to the ground all across the planet.

Stepping outside, you smell that distinct earthy aroma that arrives after freshly fallen rain. There is a technical term for this smell, called *petrichor*, and it's a combination of the Greek words for "rock" or "stone" and "ichor," the fluid the Greek gods had in their veins instead of blood. A whiff of this may have you just as energized as those ancient Olympians.

And beyond the petrichor, the cool, crisp air fills your lungs and focuses your senses. If you love the fresh feeling of the air right after a rainstorm, it may have something to do with the fact that it's so clean; just 1 inch (2.5 cm) of rain can scrub virtually all airborne particulates from the air, along with nasty gasses like sulfur dioxide.

So the next time you think one of these big, lumbering nimbostratus clouds has ruined your plans for the day, just wait for the rain to pass—and be thankful instead!

MINDFUL REFLECTION

Often our most difficult moments can be our best teachers. Reflect on a situation or event that was challenging for you. How did you feel during the event? How have you grown or changed after this experience?

ALTOSTRATUS

A s the name would imply, an altostratus cloud is a mid-level version of the low, gray stratus cloud commonly found between 6,000 and 16,000 feet (1,800 and 4,800 m). An altostratus typically exhibits even fewer visible structures or patterns than a stratus does—if you can see any variation in shades of gray at all, you're most likely looking at a stratus.

Indeed, the description of altostratus clouds makes it seem like their only distinct quality is a *lack* of distinct qualities. They don't have patterns or shapes. They're mostly uniform gray. Most of the time, they don't produce precipitation. And they can extend over several thousands of square miles and just hang out in the sky, being boring.

What is interesting about the altostratus, though, is not necessarily itself—but rather how it can affect and play with light sources. All altostratus clouds block enough of the light of the sun or moon that shadows completely vanish from the landscape. Instead, that light is scattered uniformly. If you happen to be observing the outdoors with a camera in hand, you may be disappointed to miss a brilliant bluebird sky or the intricate structures of some of the other cloud types, but know that many photographers treasure the humble altostratus for its ability to create that uniform, diffused light. This setting is great for portraits because it can soften the look of the skin, it provides some dynamic range if you're taking photographs of naturally lit interiors, and the flattened range of light can work wonders for outdoor photographers, too.

While a gray sky may not sound like the most illuminating and revealing outdoor setting, use this time to look again at some of your favorite places or things. If your eyes are usually drawn toward showy blooms in a garden, an altostratus may instead let them wander toward the now-highlighted variegation of the leaves and stems. When everything around you is evenly lit, you'll be surprised what can pop out at you.

There are other ways altostratus can play with light in interesting ways. In an *opacus* variety of altostratus, the sky is completely uniform gray. In a *translucidus* variety, however, you will be able to see the outline of the sun or moon behind the clouds. If the translucidus variety is thin enough, it may create an eerie, solid disc of light around the outline of the sun or moon called a *corona* (meaning "crown" in Latin). Thin layers may also organize into shadowy bands that look like the bottom of waves, called *undulatus*, which can make for some extremely meditative cloud-gazing.

An altostratus cloud usually begins as a higher cirrostratus (page 75) that thickens when a warmer layer of air rises above it and pushes the cloud layer down. As it descends, it may gather enough moisture to become a rain-producing nimbostratus. But if it maintains its drier composition, it will become an altostratus cloud, which will put on an impressive visual show in the right conditions.

If there is clear air behind them at sunset or sunrise, and if the sun's rays aren't being blocked by lower layers of clouds, for a very brief time these otherwise drab and unremarkable altostratus clouds will absolutely explode in reddish hues, from light pink to almost fire engine red. With the sun hitting the clouds at an angle, you may also finally be able to see the otherwise hidden patterns and structures inside the altostratus. Looking up at such a display, you would be hard-pressed to use the word "unremarkable" to describe it.

ALTOSTRATUS

MINDFUL
REFLECTION

Try looking at or thinking
about something extremely
commonplace as if you've
never encountered it before.
What is truly wonderful
about this object? What else
can you look at differently?

ALTOCUMULUS

The altocumulus is a mid-level cloud that usually appears as clumps or rolls. They are fair-weather clouds that float peacefully in calm or stable air currents, which means they can persist as a single layer of cloud without changing all that much over time. But if that description has you thinking these clouds aren't fascinating to observe, think again.

Unlike the cumulus and cumulonimbus clouds that are formed and fueled by thermal air currents, the much calmer altocumulus form high enough in the atmosphere that they are usually outside the influence of those convection engines. Instead, they appear after the gradual dissolution of an altostratus from the sun's rays, or by pockets of moist air that have been lifted and cooled by gentle currents.

They appear as "cloudlets" that form into clusters. They can be white or gray, and unlike cirrocumulus clouds (which generally don't appear to have shading due to their higher elevation and ice crystal content), altocumulus clouds are shaded on the side facing away from the sun. The lower stratocumulus clouds are usually much darker.

Even though they tend to be pretty relaxed as far as clouds go, what they lack in convective action, they make up for in sheer variety. Altocumulus clouds can appear in seven different varieties and fall into three species. If they stretch over a large area of sky instead of forming clumps or patches, they're called *stratiformis*. If their top layer rises in little columns and turrets, they're called *castellanus*. Rougher cloudlets that look like miniature cumulus clouds with uneven bases are called *flocus*. And the last species, *Lenticularis*, is sometimes called a UFO.

The *Altocumulus lenticularis* looks similar to the stratocumulus cloud of the same variety because it's formed in the same manner—by moist air being forced upward as it hits the slope of a hill or mountain. The way to tell the difference between the two is that the altocumulus looks smooth, while the stratocumulus has a rougher appearance. The *lenticularis* varieties of clouds are called orographic clouds, and because they depend upon hills and mountains to form, they can often be found in hilly or mountainous regions, though they are somewhat more reliably spotted in areas where mountains have a good degree of prominence—like the isolated volcanic peaks of the Cascade Range.

Here, as moist air flows eastward from the Pacific Ocean, peaks like Mount Hood can often be found sporting a cap of *Altocumulus lenticularis*, even when the air around is cloud-free (these are sometimes referred to as *Cap and Banner clouds*—*cap* for when a summit is obscured and *banner* for when a cloud seems to be flying in one direction). It's not always the case, but sometimes *lenticularis* clouds achieve an almost perfectly round shape, and can appear to be disguised flying saucers, if that's where your cloud-spotting imagination takes you.

Your mind may wander quite a bit when viewing *Altocumulus flocus* as well. These rough-textured altocumulus clouds usually show up in humid, unstable air, and if you see them during the evening, there's a good chance the next morning may be stormy. But in the meantime, keep your eye on the lower stretches of these clouds. You may be lucky enough to see long trails of misty-looking leg formations beneath them. These are called *virga*, and are rain or snow that evaporates before it hits the ground. Virga give the clouds an otherworldly appearance, and it's easy to imagine them as giant floating jellyfish slowly making their way across the sky.

MINDFUL
REFLECTION

Often, two things we think of
as very distinct have more
in common than we may
notice at first glance. Instead
of looking for differences,
look for similarities. Think of
two or more wildly different
objects and find their
common bonds. How are you
the same as a houseplant?
How is a fork like a raven?

CUMULONIMBUS

Some clouds announce themselves by light (or lack thereof). Other clouds may announce themselves with rain. Only one cloud can announce itself with sound—sound that may rattle your windows or send your pets fleeing to your bedside for comfort.

The cumulonimbus cloud is huge—by far the largest of clouds. They generally begin about 2,000 feet (600 m) off the ground and continue towering above until they reach the edge of the troposphere (the first layer of the Earth's atmosphere), which, depending on where you are and what season it is, can be up to 65,000 feet (20,000 m). For scale, the summit of Mount

Everest sits at a comparatively modest 29,032 feet (8,849 m).

The same type of thermal energy that feeds the growth of cumulus clouds is responsible for birthing these noisy sky beasts. A large *Cumulus congestus* cloud may look similar, but when the sharply defined outlines on the tops of those clouds turn brighter and softer—a result of the cloud reaching those upper limits of the troposphere and its water droplets turning to ice—then it has officially become a cumulonimbus cloud. It's called *Cumulonimbus calvus* if that upper portion is in flattened mounds, and *Cumulonimbus capillatus* if it looks messy or indistinct or has an anvil-like shape to it.

Conditions do need to be just right for these giants to grow, though. First, they need a supply of warm, moist air, which, when drawn into thermal updrafts, fuels the growth of the cloud's enormous convection engine. Second, the winds need to increase in speed *in the direction* the cloud is moving as the height of the cloud increases. This gives the cumulonimbus cloud a distinct, forward-slant-ing appearance and prevents the cold down-drafts and large hailstones inside the cloud from destroying the formation. Lastly, the air around the cloud needs to become cooler with increased altitude. This is generally true anywhere you'd find a cloud, but the tempera-ture difference is larger in subtropical environ-ments, which is why those regions tend to get more thunderstorms.

The energy created by these clouds is astounding. By some measures, it is estimated to be about ten times the amount of energy released by an early atomic bomb. Hopefully you are not directly beneath this cloud while you are observing it. Not only would you likely be drenched in heavy downpours of rain and hail, but you would also be in danger of getting struck by lightning. And from an observational standpoint, you wouldn't really see much of the cloud itself.

Despite their massive size and monstrous energy, a single cumulonimbus cloud doesn't live for very long. Meteorologists describe

storm clouds like the cumulonimbus as cells—
and a single cell cloud may only last about
an hour. More commonly, though, you'll see
a new cumulonimbus cloud forming off the
dissipating energy of another, which is called
a multicell storm. Multicell storms that form
over warm seas, stretch hundreds of miles, and
rage on for a full day are called supercells.

Perhaps more than any other cloud, the
cumulonimbus is an exemplar of change. Not
only does the cloud itself offer a fascinating
light and sound show and demonstrable evi-
dence of convection currents, but the change it
brings to those of us on the ground is palpable.

Think of a sticky, humid summer day—
one where it may be difficult to walk around
or even breathe. You watch the clear yellow-
and-red band on local weather radar that signals a front moving into your area. Suddenly
the sky darkens; rain pounds on your rooftop.
Flashes of lightning are followed by the roll-
ing rumble of thunder as the storm passes.

Then, the sky clears. Maybe the sun even
returns. If you open your window, you might

be surprised by a blast of cooler, drier air and the sound of birds returning after the meteorological maelstrom.

If you happen to live in a part of the world that experiences monsoon storms, this effect will be even more pronounced. In the Sonoran Desert of the American Southwest, the air may be so dry that even the powerful downpours of a cumulonimbus cloud evaporate before reaching the ground, creating the appearance of long, wispy virgas. If the rain does reach the desert floor, though, it comes down hard and fast. Arroyos and dry riverbeds roar to life, canyons may be filled with flash floods that can carve new channels, and lingering runoff may provide new habitats for desert spadefoot toads or fuel for an ocotillo's vigorous but short-lived green growth.

These drastic changes are all in a day's (or hour's) work for these enormous, majestic clouds.

CUMULONIMBUS

MINDFUL
REFLECTION

Change can happen
suddenly, and sometimes
it can feel chaotic and
dangerous. Remember that
the storm—like the calm
before—only lasts so long.
Strive to appreciate both
states without clinging
to the calm or recoiling
from the chaos.

CIRROSTRATUS

T he cirrostratus cloud is a high-altitude formation. Delicate and thin, it is comprised of ice crystals that spread over vast areas of sky.

Cirrostratus clouds usually form when a number of more grainy-appearing cirrus clouds spread out or are joined together. You'll often see the two forms together at the same time, but the cirrostratus is a more continuous layer than the cirrus clouds are. Although they can be huge in terms of area, they can go unnoticed by most people due to their slight and subtle form—even though they can also create unusual and dramatic visual effects.

In their least dramatic form, cirrostratus clouds may appear as only an indistinct milkiness in the sky. Sunlight and moonlight can pass through, and unlike the altostratus clouds, you will still most often be able to see shadows on the ground. This species of altostratus is called *nebulosis*, which indicates the cloud layer is smooth with no variation in color. The sky may even appear to be a regular, clear blue sky, but perhaps you may perceive it as being a bit hazy.

If the cirrostratus cloud is being hit by consistent high-speed winds—a not-uncommon occurrence at this high altitude—then this fine, delicate layer may become frayed-looking, with thin, parallel wisps that look like the tattered edge of your favorite sweater. This species is known as *fibratus*.

In addition to noticing and appreciating these fine strands of cloud, which are so delicate they seem like you could disintegrate them with a single puff of breath, take note that the cirrostratus cloud can also be a sign of changing weather conditions if observed over a longer time period.

If the cirrostratus layer appears to spread out and cover more area of sky as it darkens, it's a sign that wet weather is likely to move into your area over the next few days (cirrostratus clouds themselves do not create any precipitation, though). Alternatively, if the day begins with a solid layer of cirrostratus and the clouds break up into cirrocumulus clouds, you can safely leave your umbrellas at home for the next day or two.

Because the cirrostratus will usually manifest as a thin, translucent layer that still lets plenty of light through *and* because it is comprised of ice crystals, this cloud type has a tendency to do some very interesting things to the sunlight or moonlight that passes through it. For one, it is known to reliably create halo phenomena—which can manifest as points of light, arcs, or even full rings around the sun or moon. Depending on the type of ice crystals in the clouds—as well as where you are observing them from—these halo effects may be seen as just slightly dimmer light or they may even have a variety of colors.

Another surprisingly common cirrostratus phenomena is known by the wonderful name *sundog*. A sundog is an optical illusion that occurs when refracting light creates points of light that appear on either or both sides of the sun, most often when the sun is lower in the horizon in the months of January, April, August, and October. And beyond seeming to create two additional suns in the sky, a sundog may also display various colors—the point closer to the sun may look red, while the point further from the sun appears yellow or white.

So the next time the sky seems maybe just a *tad* hazier than its usual bright shade of blue, take a moment or two to enjoy a closer look at what's going on above you.

MINDFUL REFLECTION

Find something that seems to have a uniform appearance from a distance. On a closer approach, what patterns or details emerge that you may have missed earlier? What other seemingly simple things are more complex than you might have guessed?

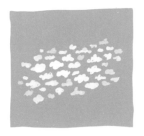

CIRROCUMULUS

I n places like the Pacific Northwest, winter can mean near-constant socked-in skies and unremarkable drizzle for weeks on end—not much to write home about. But other locations can get reliable bright blue days in the cold air. And careful eyes turned skyward may see a faint, almost imperceptible layer of clouds floating peacefully high up in the atmosphere.

The cirrocumulus cloud is composed almost entirely of ice crystals, and although it may appear to be a single smooth layer like the cirrostratus, the cirrocumulus is distinct in that it is comprised of tiny *cloudlets* rather than a single layer. These cloudlets may actually be quite large—but because they are so far away from you on the ground (some cirrocumulus clouds can reach altitudes of 45,000 feet [13,700 m]), they may be small and numerous enough to look like a single layer. If cirrus clouds (page 85) are graceful paintbrush swaths, then the cirrocumulus is perhaps the spackle of a popcorn ceiling.

Cirrocumulus clouds have three primary species. If these tiny, high flying dots are spread out over a large chunk of sky, they care called *stratiformis*. If the tops of the cloudlets have turret formations—which you honestly may not be able to see unless you have binoculars—they are called *castellanus*. Cirrocumulus clouds also come in *floccus*—small-looking cumulus formations with rough bases and virga formations—as well as the flying saucer *lenticularis* species, although the direct influence of the terrain is tougher to see on the cirrocumulus versions because they tend to be so high above the hills and mountains that trigger them.

It may be tough to tell the species of cirrocumulus from ground level, but there are two varieties that are generally easier to distinguish. The *undulatus* variety is when this layer's cloudlets gather up into wave formations. The *lacunosis* variety is more of a lattice framework of cloudlets assembled around distinctive holes.

Cirrocumulus clouds tend not to stick around for very long. The patches and cloudlets of cirrocumulus usually appear alongside cirrus and cirrostratus clouds because they often serve as the transitional form between those other forms. If you spot the grainy formations of cirrocumulus, consider yourself lucky; they may have melted into the wispy forms of the cirrus the next time you look up.

Although the cirrocumulus usually shows up in fair, cold weather, if a *Cirrocumulus stratiformis* layer is covering up a huge area overhead, it is sometimes called a "mackerel sky" and might signify the onset of bad weather. This is a reference to an old seafaring saying: "Mare's tails and mackerel scales make tall ships carry low sails." In this case, "mare's tails" are referring to cirrus clouds, and "mackerel scales" to cirrocumulus. If there is a large area of this mackerel sky overhead, it means the high troposphere has a large amount of moisture in it. And while cirrocumulus clouds themselves don't create any precipitation, if this moisture drops lower, it can turn into rain-producing clouds. Additionally, the small cloudlet formations of the cirrocumulus can indicate fast moving, unstable winds at that level, which could suggest a strong approaching storm front.

In case you were wondering what *kind* of mackerel, exactly, this mackerel sky is, don't worry. In his informative and entertaining book *The Cloudspotter's Guide*, author Gavin Pretor-Pinney went to a local fish market in London's East End to compare scales firsthand. His determination? Mackerel sky is named after the king mackerel.

CIRROCUMULUS

MINDFUL REFLECTION

Unlike the changes wrought by
the cumulonimbus cloud, the
cirrocumulus tends to shift
into different forms almost
without notice. We, too, can be
distracted enough to not notice
changes occurring in our own
lives. Check in with yourself at
regular intervals throughout the
day and notice what's going on.
How have you changed since
this morning? How will you
change before the day is done?

CIRRUS

C irrus clouds are the highest clouds in the sky, reaching altitudes of 20,000 to 40,000 feet (6,000 to 12,000 m). Comprised entirely of ice crystals at the height of the troposphere, cirrus clouds are a common cloud type that is distinctively wispy and fragile looking. But like many things, the appearances of these clouds from ground level obscures some of the most interesting aspects about them.

Appearing as bright white, lightly painted brushstrokes against the sky, cirrus clouds are known for their unique fibrous formations called fallstreaks. They are rarely thick enough to block out the sun, and in the right position, nearly all cirrus formations have the ability to create halo phenomena around the sun or moon.

Created by the ascent of dry air, the cirrus clouds are formed when that small amount of moisture reaches the colder temperatures at the upper troposphere. And although they may look stationary, these most delicate of cloud formations are being constantly buffeted by winds that reach speeds of up to 150 miles per hour (240 km per hour). In fact, cirrus clouds are the fastest-moving cloud type—they just appear slow-moving to us all the way down on the surface of the Earth.

Cirrus clouds come in five different species. If a cirrus cloud is seen without any hooks or clumps at the end of its fallstreak, they are known as *fibratus*. *Cirrus fibratus* clouds are generally aligned with the direction of the high-altitude wind. Fallstreaks that end in bent shapes that appear as hooks or commas are called *uncinus*. (In the old mariner's saying about the altocumulus "mackerel sky," the "mare's tails" are *Cirrus uncinus*.) *Castellanus* refers to cirrus clouds that are wider than they are tall. *Flocus* are fallstreaks from individual rounded clouds that may look more cottony than other cirrus clouds. Finally, the *Cirrus spissatus* is a larger, thick patch of cirrus cloud that can be formed from a passing warm front or the remnants of the top of a cumulonimbus that's exhausted itself.

Cirrus clouds may easily go unnoticed by most folks on solid ground, but taking the time to watch individual clouds in our upper troposphere can be most rewarding. The fallstreaks may seem to dance in slow motion, swaying with the high winds or becoming twisted into tangled and bent shapes. In some instances, the fallstreaks may seem to arrange themselves in regimented parallel lines or stretch out toward the horizon. Like other high-altitude clouds, they can most definitely put on a show at sunrise or sunset, when the light strikes them from a lower angle.

If you happen to be thoughtfully observing a set of high cirrus clouds in flux alongside their common high-altitude companions the cirrocumulus and cirrostratus clouds, you may also be witness—over a longer period of time—to a common and well-worn cloud progression that signals some oncoming rain.

Watch the cirrus clouds in motion and note the direction of wind around you at surface level. If you stand with the wind at your back and the cirrus clouds are moving to the right, that's a sign that a low pressure system is moving into the area. Now, over the next few days (and hopefully from the comfort of the indoors), you can watch as the delicate cirrus clouds slowly coalesce into cirrostratus. These then gradually lower and fill with more moisture from the upper levels of the troposphere, becoming first altostratus (with some potential light rain) and later nimbostratus (with some longer-lasting and heavier rainfall). Once the clouds have spent their moisture, the nimbostratus will settle into a gray, all-encompassing stratus before thermals (columns of warm air rising from the earth) start driving the convection engines that create stratocumulus and cumulus clouds, finally revealing some blue sky again.

CIRRUS

MINDFUL
REFLECTION

Try to find a single cirrus
cloud in the sky. Get
comfortable and watch it for
as long as you can—ideally
until it dissolves or moves
into another cloud form.
What does it look like at each
step? How is it changing
and moving?

HAMLET: Do you see yonder cloud that's almost in shape of a camel?

POLONIUS: By the mass, and 'tis like a camel, indeed.

HAMLET: Methinks it is like a weasel.

POLONIUS: It is backed like a weasel.

HAMLET: Or like a whale.

POLONIUS: Very like a whale.

—William Shakespeare, *Hamlet*

IV.

UNIQUE PHENOMENA

Perhaps you have had the experience of looking up into the sky and thinking, "Wait, what is THAT?" In addition to the ten common types of clouds listed in the previous section, there are plenty of unique cloud-spotting marvels to appreciate.

Whether unusual varieties of clouds, members of a separate cloud family known as *accessory clouds*, or phenomena triggered by the angle of light or the amount of ice crystals or water droplets in the atmosphere, the sky can show us humans on the ground some pretty amazing things. This is by no means an exhaustive list, but it is a little something to get you started (and maybe answer that

question you had when you looked upward
and saw something that caught your eye).

These varieties may appear in different genera
and species of other clouds, but do tend to be
show-stoppers once noticed.

Radiatus

The term *radiatus* comes from the Latin
meaning "to be radiant" or "to have rays," and
describes what happens when a group of
clouds or cloudlets seems to arrange itself into
neat, straight, almost parallel lines. These lines
form with the direction of the winds. The
radiatus variety can be found in altocumulus,
altostratus, cirrus, cumulus, and stratocumulus
clouds, but is perhaps most dramatic in cumulus and cirrus. If a cumulus cloud grouping
is in the radiatus variety, they are sometimes
known as *cloud streets*, and present as rows
of little puffy cotton balls marching off into

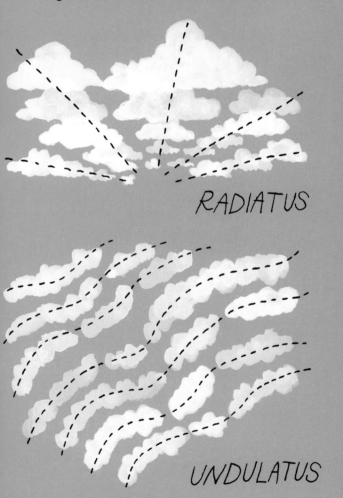

CLOUD VARIETIES

RADIATUS

UNDULATUS

the distance. If higher-level cirrus clouds are caught up in the furious winds of a jet stream, their delicate forms can be rushed off into the distant horizon in consecutive straight lines, where, to the human eye, they meet to form a sort of sunburst pattern.

Undulatus

From the Latin term for "wave," *undulatus* is an apt term for this variety of cloud, which can appear like the rippled surface of a choppy pond or perhaps the sand left behind on a sandbar at low tide. These are formed when the air above and below a cloud layer are moving at different speeds or in different directions, and are common enough to be found in six genera of cloud—altocumulus, altostratus, cirrocumulus, cirrostratus, stratocumulus, and stratus.

ACCESSORY AND OTHER CLOUDS

These clouds don't necessarily fit in with the other genera—or they may be special names

94

given to clouds that only appear in certain circumstances.

Cap and Banner

Both cap and banner clouds form near prominent mountain summits, and they are kind of exactly what you'd expect by these names. Cap clouds are types of lenticular clouds that sit on top of a mountain summit, obscuring it. Banner clouds form when a wind blows across the peak. The air pressure behind the peak drops and cools, allowing a cloud to form there when one may not be present on the other side. The result is that the mountain peak looks like it's flying a long cloud flag from its summit.

Kelvin-Helmholtz

These fancy-sounding clouds (named for Lord Kelvin and Hermann von Helmholtz, who studied the conditions that lead to this formation) are some of the rarest and most fleeting clouds in the sky. Like the undulatus varieties, these are formed when two air

ACCESSORY & OTHER CLOUDS

BANNER

KELVIN-HELMHOLTZ

MAMMATUS

PILEUS

PYROCUMULUS

masses moving at differing speeds pile on top of each other and present as a row of almost cartoonish wave formations in the sky. They don't last very long—usually only a few minutes—but you have a better chance of seeing them near sunrise or sunset on windy days, especially during an inversion when warmer air rests on top of a cooler layer.

Mammatus

Mammatus comes from the Latin term for "udder" or "breast," and these huge and dramatic formations do appear to hang down from an upper layer of cloud like a cow's udders. They can be found on a wide range of cloud formations but tend to grab the most attention when they form on the underside of the anvil-shaped *incus* formations of the cumulonimbus cloud. They tend to only last about ten minutes or so, and generally are found behind storms, not in front of them— so if there's a menacing thundercloud in the neighborhood and you see mammatus, odds are the bad weather has already passed you by.

Pileus

Pileus means "cap" in Latin, and these accessory clouds form much in the same manner as the cap cloud—the only difference is that instead of forming above a mountain or hill, pileus clouds form over other clouds! These smooth, rounded white layers typically form above cumulonimbus or cumulus congestus clouds, and they only last a few moments.

Pyrocumulus

A pyrocumulus cloud is a cumulus cloud that forms above a fire or volcanic eruption if there is enough moisture in the air and the fire or eruption has kicked up enough soot or ash for water droplets to bond to and form a cloud. If the fire or eruption is large enough, a pyrocumulus cloud may even produce lightning and thunder or precipitation.

Some other interesting things you may notice while cloud spotting.

Bows

We've likely all seen rainbows before. They are most likely to show up around convection clouds like the *Cumulus congestus* and cumulonimbus, which produce rain but still leave enough space in the cloud cover for sunlight to get through. We may not be as familiar with their close cousins cloudbows and fogbows though. A fogbow looks like a rainbow in grayscale, and shows up when you are looking into thin fog or mist with the sun behind you. A cloudbow is a bit tougher to see, but forms in the same scenario, just in a cloud rather than fog. The tricky thing with cloudbows is that you usually have to be above the cloud layer to see them, so put on those hiking boots!

Glory

When your shadow is cast directly on top
of a cloud, that is known as a *glory*. When it
appears, you will see your shadow encircled
by series of rainbow rings. Since you need to
be looking down at a cloud, this phenomenon
requires you to be at a high elevation. You
have a fairly decent chance of seeing this
from looking out the window of an airplane,
but you can also experience this on top of a
mountain ridge looking down at lower layers
of clouds while the sun is behind you. A
glory seen from a mountaintop is known as
a *Brocken spectre*, named for Brocken peak in
Germany's Harz Mountains where this phenomenon frequently occurs.

OTHER PHENOMENA

FOGBOW

GLORY

DO CONTRAILS COUNT?

A contrail—short for *condensation trail*—is the straight line of condensation that forms immediately behind the engines of high-altitude jet aircraft. Meteorologists and cloud spotters do consider these formations clouds, as they are comprised of the same stuff every other cloud is made up of—water vapor, droplets, ice, and particles. The only difference between a contrail and other clouds is that contrails are created by human activity.

Contrails appear as straight lines high in the sky at airlines' cruising altitudes—generally between 28,000 and 40,000 feet (8,500 and 12,000 m). They don't always appear behind jets, though—the air at that altitude has to be cool and humid for contrails to develop. If it's too warm or dry, the ice crystals that form from the exhaust sublimate directly into water vapor. If contrails don't follow an airplane, it may be because the top of the troposphere is dry enough to indicate fair weather for the next day. Alternatively, contrails that linger and spread into a large cirrostratus layer can indicate an advancing warm front and potential precipitation.

Scientists are interested in the formation and lingering nature of persistent contrails because—like any cloud—they affect the atmosphere. High cirrus clouds like contrails don't block a lot of sunlight but they will trap heat radiating back from the surface, so contrails can directly increase the temperature in a given area.

The Federal Aviation Administration has tracked the percentage of cloud cover from contrails and found—unsurprisingly—that they tend to appear where flight patterns are the most dense, namely in the continental United States and Western Europe. Although contrails pose no direct threat to human health or safety, many groups are considering ways to decrease the creation of contrails in flight paths to limit these additional heat-trapping clouds. Some potential solutions include increasing fuel efficiency in aircraft engines and potentially lowering flight paths to reduce the chances that contrails will form behind planes.

REST is not idleness,
and to lie sometimes
ON THE GRASS UNDER TREES
on a summer's day,
listening to the
MURMUR of the water.
Or watching the CLOUDS
FLOAT ACROSS THE SKY,
is by no means a
waste of TIME.

—John Lubbock, *The Use of Life*

V.

ATTACHMENT

Before we go—and leave you to a wonderful time spent staring at the sky—it is worth taking a short moment to talk about one of the most important aspects of mindfulness: attachment.

Living free of attachments does not mean you have to live the life of a monk, deep in the mountains with no human contact. Nor does it mean you have to live a life of austerity, subsisting only on tea and dry crackers. The aim of living free of attachments is to allow yourself to be comfortable with the ever-changing, impermanent nature of the world.

As we mentioned earlier, the act of observing and learning more about clouds might actually be one of the best ways to learn about approaching the world without a sense of attachment. You may find the form of a wind-whipped cirrus cloud to be particularly beautiful, but odds are its form will completely change if you look back up at it in a moment or two.

The goal here is not to mourn the loss of the shape you found particularly enchanting, but rather to just enjoy and appreciate it while it exists in your consciousness. And—ideally—you can also appreciate and enjoy whatever form follows. Eventually, you may find this new mindset creeping into other parts of your life too.

You just learned a ton of information about clouds. You know what their forms are, what their names are in Latin, and even some of the systems that drive types of clouds or what kinds of weather they may predict in the future. And if any of that sticks around in your brain and comes to the surface when you're observing a cloud formation—wonderful!

But also, don't feel like you need to remember every single genus, species, and variety in Latin when you're observing cloud formations. It's totally OK if you don't remember the cloud you're looking at is an *Altocumulus floccus* with virga formations. Maybe you just remember it's an altocumulus. Or maybe you just think of it as that pretty cloud formation backlit by the sun with interesting jellyfish tentacles coming out of its base. All three of those observations are completely valid—and hey, no one should ever be discouraged from finding hidden animals in clouds.

Happy cloud spotting!

Cloud Appreciation Ltd. "Cloud Appreciation Society." Cloud Appreciation Society. Updated November 16, 2021. https://cloudappreciationsociety.org

Coleman, Mark. "Awake in the Wild: Mindfulness in Nature as a Path of Self Discovery." Novato: New World Library, 2006.

Day, John A. "The Book of Clouds." New York City: Sterling, 2005.

Hamblyn, Richard. "The Cloud Book: How to Understand the Skies." Cincinnati: David and Charles Limited, 2008.

Hanh, Thich Nhat. "The Miracle of Mindfulness: an Introduction to the Practice of Meditation." Boston: Beacon Press, 1976.

Kabat-Zinn, Jon. "Wherever You Go, There You Are: Mindfulness Meditation in Everyday Life." New York City: Hachette Books, 2005.

Met Office, The. "Clouds." The Met Office. Updated November 16, 2021. https://www.metoffice.gov.uk/weather/learn-about/weather/types-of-weather/clouds

Pretor-Pinney, Gavin. "The Cloud Collector's Handbook." San Francisco: Chronicle Books, 2011.

Pretor-Pinney, Gavin. "The Cloudspotter's Guide: The Science, History, and Culture of Clouds." New York City: Penguin Group, 2006.

CASEY SCHREINER is an author, a television writer and producer, and the founder of modernhiker.com. He splits his time between Los Angeles, California, and Portland, Oregon. Find more of his work at caseyschreiner.com.

SEE MORE BOOKS IN THE SERIES

THE POCKET NATURE SERIES offers meditative and insightful guides to reconnecting with the natural world through mindful practices.

WWW.CHRONICLEBOOKS.COM/POCKETNATURE